# MY BOOK OF
# 1-MINUTE STORIES
## AND VERSES

NEW YORK

# CONTENTS

Cover illustration by Carol Pike

Cover design by Kasa and Steel

Copyright © Marshall Cavendish 1982, 1983, 1984
This edition © 1987 by Marshall Cavendish Limited

First published in USA 1987 by Exeter Books
Distributed by Bookthrift
Exeter is a trademark of Bookthrift Marketing, Inc.
Bookthrift is a registered trademark of Bookthrift Marketing, Inc.
New York, New York

ALL RIGHTS RESERVED

ISBN 0-671-08500-X

Printed and bound in Vicenza, Italy by L.E.G.O.

# I Had a Little Nut Tree

I had a little nut-tree,
　Nothing would it bear
But a silver nutmeg
　And a golden pear.

The King of Spain's daughter
　Came to visit me,
All for the sake
　Of my little nut-tree.

I skipped over ocean,
　I danced over sea;
And all the birds in the air
　Couldn't catch me!

There were once three tortoises — a father, a mother and a baby. And one fine spring day they decided that they would like to go for a picnic. They chose the place they would go to, a nice wood some distance off, and began to get their stuff together. They got tins of salmon and tins of tongue, and sandwiches, and orange squash, and everything they could think of. In about three months they were ready, and they set out, carrying their baskets on their backs.

They walked and walked and walked, and time went on, and after about eighteen months they sat down and had a rest. But they knew just where they wanted to go and they were about half-way to it, so they set out again. And in three years they reached the picnic place. They unpacked their baskets and spread out the cloth, and arranged the food on it, and it looked lovely.

Then Mother Tortoise began to look into the picnic baskets. She turned them all upside down, and shook them, but they were all empty, and at last she said, "We've forgotten the tin opener!" They looked at each other, and at last Father and Mother said, "Baby, you'll have to go back for it."

# The Tortoises' Picnic

"What!" said the baby. "Me! Go back all that long way?"

"Nothing for it," said Father Tortoise. "We can't start without a tin-opener. We'll wait for you."

"Well, do you swear, do you promise faithfully," said the baby, "that you won't touch a thing till I come back?"

"Yes, we promise faithfully," they said. So Baby plodded away, and after a while he was completely lost to sight among the bushes.

And Father and Mother waited. They waited and waited and waited, and a whole year went by, and they began to get rather hungry. But they had promised, so they waited. And another year went by, and another, and they got really very hungry.

"Don't you think we could have just one sandwich each?" said Mother Tortoise. "He ought to be back by now."

"Yes, I suppose he ought," said Father Tortoise. "Let's just have one sandwich — while we're waiting."

They picked up the sandwiches, but just as they were going to eat them, a little voice said, "Aha! I knew you'd cheat." And Baby Tortoise popped his head out of a bush. "It's a good thing I didn't start for that tin-opener," he said.

In a terraced house between the gasworks and the railway station, lived a very miserable man. He was miserable because he lived between a motor-bike mechanic and a music teacher.

Every morning, the man was woken by the mechanic hammering and banging and clanging and revving away on motor-bikes in the yard. It seemed as if the noise would shake the house down.

Then the first pupil would arrive at the music teacher's house, and there would be a screeching of violins, or a thundering of pianos, or a caterwauling of trumpets, or the ear-splitting whine of a flute played flat. It seemed as if the music would break every window in the middle house.

The man living between these noisy neighbours tried everything — ear-plugs, ear-muffs, putting his head under the pillow, even locking himself in the cupboard. But the engines revved and the music jangled, until he thought his head would burst.

NOISY

"This just can't go on," he thought to himself one morning. But he could not hear himself think, so he had to shout it aloud instead. *"This can't go on!"*

So he went next door to the mechanic's house and offered him a fistful of money if he would sell his house and move.

"Anything you say, chief!" said the mechanic, who had never held so much money in his oily hands. "I'll move out tomorrow!"

Then the man went to his other neighbour, the music teacher, and offered her all the money he had left if she would sell her house and move.

"Oh, of course, absolutely my dear!"

# NEIGHBOURS

said the teacher, who had never seen so much money in her life. "I'll move tomorrow!"

So the man from the middle house went home happy and locked himself in the cupboard with his ear-plugs and a pillow over his head for the last time.

And he wondered why he had never thought of the remedy before.

Next morning, he even went round to help the music teacher pack.

"I hope you've found somewhere nice to live," he said as he helped her carry the piano downstairs.

"Oh, yes than you. I was really very lucky. I found out that the motor-bike mechanic who lives two doors away was also looking for somewhere else to live. So I'm moving into his house

. . . and he's moving into mine!"

7

# The Nightingale

There was once a nightingale who lived in a large crystal cage. She belonged to a rich Persian merchant who loved, more than anything else, to listen to her sweet song. If he sometimes detected a sad note, he quickly dismissed it from his thoughts.

"My nightingale has everything a bird could possibly want," he told himself. "I'm sure she's the happiest bird in Persia."

One day the merchant announced that he was going on a long journey to buy silks and perfumes from the East. On the way he would pass the nightingale's first home — a forest whose floor was carpeted with flowers. Was there anything the nightingale wished him to say to her brothers and sisters?

"Just tell them I'm well," she said, "and ask if they have a message for me."

The merchant did as she requested, and on returning from his journey, he immediately went to see her.

"I asked one of your brothers if he had a message for you," he said in a puzzled voice. "But all he did was to fall to the ground and lie completely still among the flowers. I picked him up, but he still didn't move, so I decided he must be dead. I gently put him down and was

just turning to leave when he fluttered his wings and flew high up into a tree. I called to him again and again to say something, but he ignored all my pleas. I think your brothers and sisters must have forgotten you."

The nightingale bowed her head in grief. All day long she refused to eat or drink any of the tasty morsels which were brought to her.

And when the merchant came to see her the next morning, he found her lying at the bottom of the cage. Not a feather moved as he begged her to fly to her perch and sing. Then he opened the cage, carefully picked her up and gently stroked her neck. But still she did not move. Stricken with grief, he thought she must have died. So, with tears in his eyes, he took her outside and laid her on the grass.

And as he walked back to his house, he turned to look at her one last time. And then he saw her brown wings quiver in the sunlight and her beak open in a cry of joy and happiness.

The nightingale soared into the sky.

"Thank you for the message from my brother," she called. "It was the best message I've ever received."

And away she flew, to the forest whose floor was carpeted with flowers.

# VIRGIL'S BIG MISTAKE

Virgil was a mean old buzzard. Nobody liked him much. He came rushing into the trading post last Spring shouting and hollering about how clever he was.

"I'm going to catch every animal on that there mountain," he cackled. "Then you'll all want to buy me a drink and slap me on the back and take my photograph."

"Have you bought yourself a new gun then, Virgil?" someone asked.

"Nope," he said. "I took my penknife and a piece of wood and I whittled myself a musical pipe, that's what I did." Everyone in the store laughed at the thought of Virgil playing music to the wild animals on the mountain. But he glared around him. "When I blow through that there pipe, I can make the noise of any animal you name — deer, racoon, beaver . . ."

"Skunk," said somebody. And Virgil stormed out of the trading post and stomped off into the Smoky Mountains with all his food *and* his musical pipe.

Well, they say he went deep among the maple trees before he took out his pipe and made the noise of a deer.

Sure enough, a little red deer heard the sound and came out of the trees. Calm as you like, Virgil loaded his gun and aimed at the little critter.

*Bang*, he took a shot at it. And he missed.

But the deer was not the only animal to hear his deer-call on the pipe. A big bobcat came down through the trees, licking his lips and thinking of deer for dinner. And when he saw old Virgil, he grinned with all his teeth.

Now, Virgil's gun was empty. But quick as a flash, he blew down the musical pipe and made the noise of a mountain lion. And he frightened that bobcat so much that he took off through the trees as fast as if a real mountain lion was on his furry heels.

But the bobcat was not the only animal to hear his lion-call on the pipe. A big hungry mountain lion came down through the trees, thinking that her mate had found something tasty for dinner. And when she saw old Virgil standing there, she grinned with all her teeth.

Quick as a flash, Virgil blew down the musical pipe again and made the noise of a great grizzly bear. And he frightened that mountain lion so bad that she took off through the trees as fast as if a real grizzly was on her furry heels.

But the mountain lion was not the only animal to hear his bear-call on the pipe. A huge lonely grizzly bear heard it and came down through the trees with love in his big grizzly heart.

But he did not find a mate. All he found was Virgil. Still, he grinned with all his teeth. And ate him up.

Well, he always was a mean old buzzard, that Virgil.

# THE DOG AND THE BONE

One day a dog sneaked into a butcher's shop and stole a fat, juicy bone. He was just slinking out of the door when he was spotted by the butcher. "You rascal," he shouted. "Come back here!"

The dog did not wait to hear any more. He began to run as fast as his legs would carry him, down the hill, over a stile and out into the country. He ran so far and so fast that he was soon very tired.

"It's no good," he panted as he reached a little bridge over a stream. "I've just got to have a rest." And, puffing hard, he stepped slowly on to the bridge.

"How refreshing that water looks," he thought, peering into the stream. "It's exactly what a hot, thirsty dog needs." And then his eyes almost popped out of his head. "That's amazing! There's a funny dog down there — and it's got a bone that's even bigger than mine."

He growled angrily. "After all I've been through, *I* deserve the biggest bone. And what's more, I'm going to have it."

He opened his mouth in a threatening snarl — but suddenly there was a huge splash. The bone had dropped straight out of his mouth and into the water.

As the water settled he saw that the dog in the stream had also lost his bone. And then he realised what had happened. "Oh no!" he whimpered. "I've been looking at a reflection of myself. How could I have been so stupid — and so greedy? Now I've got no bone at all!"

# FATHER WILLIAM

"You are old, Father William," the young man said,
    "And your hair has become very white;
And yet you incessantly stand on your head —
    Do you think, at your age, it is right?"

"In my youth," Father William replied to his son,
    "I feared it might injure the brain;
But now that I'm perfectly sure I have none,
    Why, I do it again and again."

"You are old," said the youth, "as I mentioned before,
    And have grown most uncommonly fat;
Yet you turned a back somersault in at the door —
    Pray, what is the reason of that?"

"In my youth," said the sage, as he shook his grey locks,
    "I kept all my limbs very supple
By the use of this ointment — one shilling the box —
    allow me to sell you a couple?"

"You are old," said the youth, "and your jaws are too weak
  For anything rougher than suet;
Yet you finished the goose, with the bones and the beak —
  Pray, how did you manage to do it?"

"In my youth," said his father, "I took to the law,
  And argued each case with my wife;
And the muscular strength which it gave my jaw,
  Has lasted the rest of my life."

"You are old," said the youth, "one would hardly suppose
  That your eye was as steady as ever;
Yet you balance an eel on the end of your nose —
  What made you so awfully clever?"

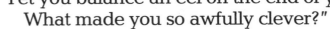

"I have answered three questions,
    and that is enough,"
Said his father. "Don't give yourself airs!
    Do you think I can listen all day to such stuff!
Be off, or I'll kick you downstairs!"

THE
FOX
AND
THE
CROW

A big, black crow was flying over a field of golden corn when she spotted some people having a picnic. They were sitting in the shade of a chestnut tree. "What a stroke of luck," she thought. "There's a good chance these people will leave me with a tasty titbit." And she glided down to perch on a branch above them.

She waited and waited, and in the end her patience was rewarded. When the picnickers packed up and walked away, they left behind a big lump of cheese. "How right I was to wait," the crow thought, as she swooped down to pick up the cheese with her beak. "How clever I am." And the crow flew back to her perch in the tree.

She was just about to start eating when a fox crept out of the cornfield. "What a delicious smell!" he said to himself, and he noisily licked his lips. His mouth watered as he raised his nose to have a good sniff. And then he saw the

crow with her lovely lump of cheese.

Now the fox was very fond of cheese. He was also very clever. "I say, crow," he said, "what a beautiful bird you are. Your feathers are so shiny, and your beak so splendidly curved, and your eyes so perfectly round." The crow was thrilled by all this flattery. She held her head high and strutted up and down the branch, hoping the fox would say more.

And the fox did say more. "A bird that looks as beautiful as you must have a wonderful voice. If only I could hear you sing, I would be happy for the rest of the day." Hearing this, the crow puffed out her chest, opened her beak, and gave a loud *caw*.

And the lump of cheese fell from the crow's mouth — and straight into the waiting jaws of the fox below.

"Than you, my dear," he said. "Now you're going to learn the price of vanity."

And then, with a chuckle, he gobbled up the piece of cheese.

# Why The Giraffe Can't Speak

Once upon a time, animal language was spoken everywhere in the forest. Giraffe, because of his long neck, was King of the Animals. Taller than all the others, he would walk about with his head in the sky and hold long conversations with himself. All the other animals were very annoyed at this, because it disturbed their afternoon peace and quiet.

So, one day they tried to think of ways to silence him. Leopard even went so far as to say, "You're not so wonderful, King Giraffe. There are lots of things you can't do that we other animals can!" "Like what?" asked Giraffe. "Well you can't run as fast as me, can you? replied Leopard. "We'll soon see about that, you impudent little cat! Let's have a race and see!" The other animals, who were certain that Leopard would win, went along to watch. Leopard and Giraffe started level, but soon Giraffe led by a neck. Then Leopard gained, overtook, and raced ahead. But then, Leopard ran into a tree, banged his head,

18

and fell to the ground. After winning the race, Giraffe grew even more vain. He walked around with his head in the air, praising himself and boasting how very much better he was than all the other animals. Soon the forest was full of Giraffe's vain chatter.

A few days later, the animals met again to decide what to do about Giraffe. But only Monkey had a plan.

He collected gum from the rubber

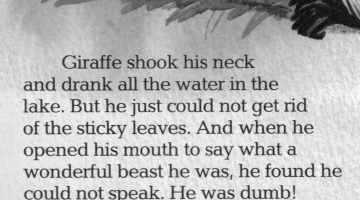

Giraffe shook his neck and drank all the water in the lake. But he just could not get rid of the sticky leaves. And when he opened his mouth to say what a wonderful beast he was, he found he could not speak. He was dumb!

All the animals thanked Monkey for silencing the boastful Giraffe. And after that they slept away every afternoon while Giraffe loped about, mouthing silent words into the topmost branches of the trees.

plant and climbed up with it into the trees. Spreading gum over every leaf, he swung from tree to tree, doing the same to each one in turn. Before very long, giraffe came by and began nibbling at the leaves.

But with every mouthful he took, the gummy leaves stuck in his long neck. And no matter how much he swallowed and coughed and swallowed, the leaves just would not move.

# THE WOLF IN SHEEP'S CLOTHING

The old wolf was as gloomy as could be. He had hurt his leg, and for a whole week now had been laid up in his lair, unable to go hunting. There was no food left at all and the wolf's stomach was rumbling furiously. To make things worse, a flock of tasty young lambs was grazing in the meadow, right under his nose!

He looked down at the remains of his last meal — just a dirty fleece and a few old bones which he had chewed a hundred times. "they don't even *smell* of food now," he moaned. And he kicked the fleece in disgust.

But at that instant, a wonderful idea came to him. "That's it! Why didn't I think of that before! If I dress up as a sheep, I won't need to hunt! I'll just crawl into the sheep-pen and choose a fat young lamb at my leisure." And he grinned from ear to ear as he draped the fleece over his shoulders.

Late that afternoon, the wolf hobbled painfully down to the meadow. He crept in amongst the flock, and waited for nightfall. And sure enough the ploy worked! The shepherd drove the wolf into the pen with all the real sheep.

But the old wolf kept his head down so low that he did not notice the big knife tucked into the shepherd's belt. The shepherd fingered the blade. "It's a long time since my family tasted fresh mutton," he was thinking. "Tonight I'll give them a feast fit for a king." With a sudden lunge, he seized the largest animal in the pen and slit its throat.

When he turned the dead animal over he saw that it was his old enemy, the wolf! The shepherd was amazed. "Well you old rogue," he chuckled. "You fooled both of us that time. But I don't think I'll be eating you for supper. You're still a wolf, whatever you're wearing."

The Wind was always boasting. "I'm stronger than anybody. I can push over trees and bury mountains in snow. I can smash ships on to rocks and tear roofs off houses. I'm stronger than anything!"

The Sun went by smiling to herself thoughtfully. "I'm stronger than you, you silly old Sun," jeered the Wind.

"Who? Me?" smiled the Sun. "Oh no, I'm afraid you're wrong, Mr Wind."

"What can you do, you over-sized orange? I challenge you to a test of strength!"

"All right," said the Sun. "Do you see that Man down there in Willow Road? He's setting off for work. I bet you can't remove his waistcoat before he catches his morning train."

The Wind hooted out loud and rolled about in a gale of laughter. "That puny thing? I'll strip him naked!"

So the Wind blew until the windows rattled in the house in Willow Road. But seeing the change in the weather, the Man hurried back indoors to snatch up his overcoat.

Then the Wind blew and blew until the Man's coat flapped round him. "Brrr! What weather!" he said, buttoning its buttons and belting its belt and hugging the collar closer round his neck.

The Wind howled and howled until the Man was struggling

# STRONGER?

against the blast.
"Brrr! What terrible
weather!" he said — and he
hopped on to a bus.
The wind roared and roared until
the bus rocked on its wheels. "Brrr! What
weather!" said the driver. "I'm taking the bus
into the depot. This wind is strong enough
to blow it over!"
So the Wind blew and howled and roared against
the depot until he went quite purple in the face.'
"Okay, know-all," it sneered at the Sun. "But I bet
you can't do any better!"
So the Sun shone. Once the Wind stopped blowing,
the bus came out of the depot and drove on towards
the station. "Phew! It's hot!" said the passengers, and got off.
The Sun shone until the Man unbuttoned his coat and mopped
his forehead. "What peculiar weather," he thought,
turning into the station yard.
The Sun shone and shone until the Man took off his jacket and
loosened his tie. "Phew! It's hot!" he said, unbuttoning his waistcoat.
The Sun beamed and beamed until the tar on the roads got sticky.
"Phew! This is too much," said the Man, and glanced around him
at the other people on the platform. They were sprawled on
seats, fanning themselves with newspapers.
"Phew!" said the Man — and he took off *his waistcoat!*
The Wind got very huffy after that. "Cheat," he muttered to the
Sun, storming off. "Man always liked you better than me!"

23

# THE BOY WHO CRIED 'WOLF'

Once there was a shepherd boy who looked after the sheep for all the people in his village. Some days it was pleasant in the hills and the time seemed to pass quickly. On the other days the boy grew bored and restless — there was nothing to do but watch the sheep nibbling at the grass from morning till night.

One day he decided to amuse himself, and he walked to the top of a crag above the village. "Help! Wolf!" he shouted at the top of his voice. "A wolf is eating the sheep!"

The moment the villagers heard the shepherd boy shouting they rushed out of their houses and up the hill to help him drive the wolf away . . . and found him laughing his head off at the trick he'd played on them. Angrily, they returned home, and the boy, still giggling, went back to watching the sheep.

A week or so later, the boy became bored again and walked to the top of the crag and shouted: "Help! Wolf! A wolf is eating the sheep!" Once again, the villagers rushed up the hill to help him. Once again, they found him laughing at their red faces and were very angry, but

there was nothing they could do except scold him.

Three weeks later the boy played exactly the same trick, and again a month after that, and yet again a few weeks after that. "Help! Wolf!" he would cry. "A wolf is eating the sheep!" Every time, the villagers dashed up the hill to help him, and every time they were met with the sight of the shepherd boy falling about with laughter over the trick he'd played on them.

Then, late one winter evening, as the boy was gathering the sheep to take them home, a wolf really *did* come prowling around the flock.

The shepherd boy was very scared. The wolf looked huge in the fading light and the boy had only his crook to fight with. He raced to the crag, yelling: "Help! Wolf! A wolf is eating the sheep!" But none of the villagers came to help the boy, for nobody believes a liar, even when he tells the truth.

"He's played that silly trick once too often," they all said. "If there *is* a wolf, then it will just have to eat the boy this time." And it did.

# My Mother Said

My Mother said, I never should
Play with gypsies in the wood.

If I did, then she would say:
"Naughty girl to disobey!

"Your hair shan't curl and your shoes shan't shine
You gypsy girl, you shan't be mine!"

And my father said that if I did,
He'd rap my head with the teapot-lid.

My mother said that I never should
Play with gypsies in the wood.

The wood was dark, the grass was green;
By came Sally with a tambourine.

I went to sea — no ship to get across;
I paid ten shillings for blind white horse.

I upped on his back and was off in a crack,
Sally tell my mother I shall never come back.

# Faster than Fairies

Faster than fairies, faster than witches,
Bridges and houses, hedges and ditches;
And charging along like troops in a battle,
All though the meadows the horses and
    cattle:
All of the sights of the hill and plain
Fly as thick as driving rain;
And ever again, in the wink of an eye,
Painted stations whistle by.

Here is a child who clambers and scrambles,
All by himself and gathering brambles;
Here is a tramp who stands and gazes;
And there is the green for stringing the
    daisies!
Here is a cart run away in the road
Lumping along with man and load;
And here is a mill and there is a river;
Each a glimpse and gone forever!

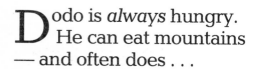

Dodo is *always* hungry. He can eat mountains — and often does . . .

One day, when Dodo was tucking into the side of a mountain, a robber saw him and thought he was digging for gold.

"Give me all your gold!" shouted the robber, pointing his gun at Dodo. "But I haven't got any . . ." said Dodo,

". . . except for the golden sunbeams. I dance on them." And Dodo did a dance on a sunbeam.

"If you can do that," said the robber, "then you can dance over the rainbow." "Of course I can," said Dodo.

"Well, there's a pot of gold at the end of the rainbow. Go and get it — or I'll blast your beak off!"

28

So Dodo danced to the top of the rainbow, with the sun shining in his eyes and the rain falling on his feathers.

Then, he slid down the other side. And there really was gold at the rainbow's end! Dodo picked it up in his beak.

But as he reached the top, the rainbow began to fade from under his feet.

Down below, the robber yelled, "Throw me the gold before the rainbow fades!"

So Dodo did. But the pot was so heavy that it *flattened* the robber . . .

. . . and all the gold spilled out in a glittering, sparkling heap. Dodo wondered what to do with it. "I could leave it here," he thought.

"But it's wrong to waste money." So he ate it.

# THE GREEDY FOX

One fine day a fox found a store of food left by some farmers inside a hollow tree. Making himself as small as he could, he squeezed through the narrow gap, so that the other animals would not be able to see him gobbling up the lovely food.

The fox ate, and ate, and ate . . . and then he ate some more. He had never eaten so much food in his life! But when he had finished it all and tried to climb out of the tree he just could not move. He was too big to get through the hole! Of course, the greedy fox did not realise he has eaten too much — he thought the tree had got smaller! He poked his head through the gap and yelled, "Help! Help! Get me out of this horrible hole."

Just then a weasel shuffled past the

tree. "Hey, weasel, help me out! This tree is shrinking. It's crushing me to death!"

"Oh, I don't think so," laughed the little weasel. "The tree looks about the same size as when I came past this morning. Perhaps you've got bigger."

"Stop talking nonsense and get me out!" shouted the fox. "I'm dying I tell you.

"Well, it serves you right for eating too much. The trouble with you is that your eyes are bigger than your stomach. You'll just have to stay there until you get thinner . . . *then* you can clamber out. And perhaps next time you won't be so greedy."

So the fox had to stay in his miserable hole for two days and two long nights. But he never ever ate too much food again.

# STONE DRUM

A chief once had a daughter called Talhulha, and the older she grew, the lovelier she became. When the chief saw this, he said to himself, "Who is worthy to be her husband?" And he himself answered, "Nobody!"

Young men brought the chief presents every day, and begged for Tahulha's hand in marriage. But though he wanted their presents, he did not want to part with his daughter. So he set a test — an impossible task for all the young men. "He who makes a drum out of stone may marry Tahulha."

When they heard this, the young men were too afraid to say, "It's impossible! No-one can do that!" So they chipped and scraped and hammered at hard, grey rocks, and tried to make a stone drum. But no-one succeeded.

Now one young man, Chilam, loved Tahulha more than the rest. So he thought longer and harder about the challenge. Each day he would leave the village, saying, "I'm going to the Place of Rocks to carve my stone drum."

Then one evening he returned to the chief's house. "I've made a stone drum," he said, "and long to play it to you, so that I may marry Tahulha. But it's heavy. Give me a cushion of smoke, so that I can carry it here on my head."

The chief stared at Chilam, then at the camp fire and its clouds of smoke billowing towards the sky. Then he called his sons, and told them, "Gather smoke!"

The boys chased the smoke, and snatched at it and tried to trap it under blankets. By they all failed.

The chief tried himself. But though he chased the smoke all round the camp and flung his cloak over it, he could not even catch one handful. "It's impossible!" he cried, wheezing and coughing and flopping down in his chair. "Why do you ask me to do what's plainly impossible? Do you mean to make a fool of your own chief?"

Then Chilam bowed deeply. "Why then did you ask the young men to make a drum of stone? That, too, is impossible. Did you mean to make a fool of your own daughter? For now she will surely grow old alone."

The chief leaped from his chair, his eyes narrow with fury. But then he saw how wise and how brave Chilam had been to say such a thing. "Tahulha!" he called. "Come and meet the husband who has won you by telling the truth. I like him. Do you think you can love him, daughter?"

Then Tahulha came out of her father's hut and took Chilam's hand. "That's not impossible," she said.

# THE OLD MAN of TORBAY

There was an old man of Torbay
Who said to his wife one day
At twelve of the clock, prepare for a shock
For I shall be floating away.

That venturesome man of Torbay
Was put in a barrel that day
They corked it up tight, and it floated upright
Far out to sea from the bay.

That nautical man of Torbay
Wobbled and rolled all the way
To strange foreign land all coral and sand
Where turtles and penguins do play.

Of that bumptious old man of Torbay
A tale shall be written one day
For a cannibal slim, did promptly cook him
And pickled that man of Torbay.

34

# I SAW A SHIP A-SAILING

I saw a ship a-sailing,
　　A-sailing on the sea;
And, oh! it was all laden
　　With pretty things for thee!

There were comfits in the cabin,
　　And apples in the hold;
The sails were made of silk,
　　And the masts were made of gold.

The four-and-twenty sailors
　　That stood between the decks,
Were four-and-twenty white mice,
　　With chains about their necks.

The captain was a duck,
　　With a jacket on his back;
And when the ship began to move,
　　The captain said, "Quack! quack!"

35

Hare was always laughing at Tortoise for being so slow. "I really can't think why you bother moving at all," he said. "Well," said Tortoise, "I may be slow, but I always get there in the end. I'll tell you what, I'll give you a race."

"You must be joking you silly slow-coach," sneered Hare. "But if you really insist . . ."
So one hot, sunny day, all the animals came to watch the Great Race. Mole lifted the starting flag and said: "Ready, Steady, *Go!*"

Hare raced away, leaving Tortoise coughing in a cloud of dust. Then Tortoise moved off — slowly, very very slowly. Hare was already out of sight.
"It's hopeless," said the Grasshoppers. "What chance does poor Tortoise have?"

"That silly Tortoise," thought Hare, looking back. "He's so slow, I can't lose. Why should I rush? In fact I think I'll just have a little rest . . ." So he lay back in the warm sun and was soon fast asleep, dreaming of cheers and prizes.

All the long morning Tortoise moved slowly, slowly along the route. Most of the animals got so bored they went home. But Tortoise just kept on going. At noon he passed Hare dozing gently by the roadside. He didn't stop to wake him. He just kept going.

Eventually, Hare woke up and stretched his legs. The sun was low in the sky. And looking back down the road, he laughed. "No sign of that silly Tortoise!" With a great leap, he raced off in the direction of the finish line to collect his prize.

But then to his horror who should he see in the distance but that silly Tortoise creeping slowly over the finish line. The flag was down. The Tortoise had won! Even from the top of the hill, Hare could hear the cheering and the clapping.

"It's not fair," whined Hare. "You cheated. Everyone knows I'm much faster than you, you old slow-coach."
"Ah," said Tortoise, looking back over his shoulder. "But I told you, I always get there in the end. Slow and steady, that's me."

The Sun and the Moon have not always lived in the sky, you know. They used to live together, husband and wife, in a huge, rambling house on the top of a hill in Africa.

They were a very friendly couple, and always welcomed visitors. They invited the Tree to tea, and she brought her cousins the Bushes. They invited the Rock and he brought his step-children, the Pebbles. The Moon invited her daughters, the Stars, to lunch and they brought along their uncles, the Planets. Indeed the parties at the house on the hill soon became very famous.

"Moon," said the Sun one morning. "We've never invited the Dew, it's high time we did."

So the Morning Dew was invited to dinner. "But I might make your lawn wet," said the Dew.

"Oh, don't worry about that. And do bring along your friends and relations if you like."

So the Dew arrived in good time for dinner — and brought her cousin the Rain. The Rain poured down on the hill until it was surrounded by water.

"I hope you don't mind," said the Rain, "but I've brought along my cousins the Ponds."

"Delighted to see you all," said the Sun, as big ponds and little ponds splashed up the garden path.

"I hope you don't mind," said the Ponds, "but we brought

along our cousins the Lakes."

"Pleased you could come," said the Moon, as grey lakes and blue lakes, deep lakes and shallow lakes rippled indoors.

"I hope you don't mind," said the Lakes, "but we brought along our friends the Rivers."

"Delighted to meet you all," said the Sun, as rushing rivers and sluggish rivers, wide rivers and bending rivers flowed up the stairs. "I hope you can all find somewhere to sit."

"I hope you don't mind," said the Rivers, "but we brought along our cousins the Estuaries."

"So nice of you all to come," said the Sun and the Moon looking at each other anxiously. "Um . . . make yourselves comfortable."

Soon the guests had filled the upstairs as well as the downstairs, and the Sun and the Moon found themselves sitting on the roof, with water lapping at their feet.

"I hope you don't mind," said the Estuaries, "but we brought along our cousins the Oceans . . ."

"Glug," said the Sun.

"Glug, glug," said the Moon. And they floated off into the sky.

And there the Sun and Moon have lived ever since, gazing down on the oceans and the rivers which crowded them out of their houses. One day, when the party is over, they might go home!

# The Silly Tortoise

One day it rained so hard that the whole country was flooded. Soon only the mountains would be left sticking up out of the floods. As the waters rose, someone could be heard crying in the valley. It was a tortoise — the slowest, silliest tortoise you have ever seen.

"Why are you crying?" honked a goose as it flew overhead.

"I'll drown!" sobbed the tortoise. "It's all right for you — you can fly. My legs are so short that it will take me days to walk all the way up the mountain. And by then the floodwaters will have washed me away."

"Come on, there's no need for all that fuss," said the goose. "I'll fetch my brother and we can take you to the mountain."

The water was up to the tortoise's neck by the time the two geese returned. They flew down holding a branch between their two beaks. The tortoise gripped the branch in his big green mouth, and the geese lifted him up into the air with a great flapping of wings.

The three of them flew over the water towards the mountain where the whole tribe of tortoises had gathered.

Every other tortoise in the land had made its way up the side of the mountain when the rain began to fall. Now they watched with delight as the two geese flew towards them, carrying the slowest, silliest tortoise. They all gave a loud cheer and began to sing in praise of the brave geese:

*"For geese are jolly good fellows*
*For geese are jolly good fellows*
*For geese are jolly good fellows . . ."*

The slowest, silliest tortoise could not help joining in. He opened his mouth and began to sing:

"AND
SO
SAY
ALL
OF
US . . ."

# A FISHY TALE

When fishes set umbrellas up
  If the rain-drops run,
Lizards will want their parasols
  To shade them from the sun.

The peacock has a score of eyes,
  With which he cannot see;
The cod-fish has a silent sound,
  However that may be.

No dandelions tell the time,
  Although they turn to clocks,
Cat's cradle does not hold the cat,
  Nor foxglove fit the fox.

The Owl and the Pussy Cat went to sea
In a beautiful pea-green boat.
They took some honey, and plenty of money
Wrapped up in a five-pound note.
The Owl looked up to the stars above,
And sang to a small guitar,
"O lovely Pussy! O Pussy, my love,
What a beautiful Pussy you are,
You are,
You are,
What a beautiful Pussy you are!"

**The Owl and the Pussy Cat**

Pussy said to the Owl, "You elegant fowl!
How charmingly sweet you sing!
O let us be married! Too long we have tarried,
But what shall we do for a ring?"
They sailed away for a year and a day,
To the land where the Bong-tree grows.
And there in a wood a Piggy-wig stood,
With a ring at the end of his nose,
His nose,
His nose,
With a ring at the end of his nose.

"Dear Pig, are you willing to sell for one shilling
Your ring?" Said the Piggy, "I will."
So they took it away, and were married next day
By the Turkey who lives on the hill.
They dined on mince and slices of quince,
Which they ate with a runcible spoon.
And hand in hand, on the edge of the sand,
They danced by the light of the moon,
The moon,
The moon,
They danced by the light of the moon.

# The ANT and the GRASSHOPPER

One glorious summer's day, a grasshopper was sitting on a blade of grass, enjoying the warmth of the sun. "This is such a lovely time of year," he said to himself. "I can't understand why everyone else is working. They should follow my example and have a good time."

Out of sheer happiness he then began to leap from one blade of grass to the next. He leapt right over a tiny black ant who was struggling to carry a grain of corn back to her store-cupboard. "Stop working so hard," cried the grasshopper. "Come and enjoy this wonderful day."

The ant looked up at him and sighed. "I'm thinking ahead," she said. "And so

should you. If you don't start storing some food now, you'll have nothing to eat in the winter." But the grasshopper laughed. "Think of the present," he called, and leapt out of sight.

One morning, a few months later, the grasshopper was creeping over the frozen ground. He was so cold and hungry that he could hardly move. As he trudged slowly past a group of ants, he saw that they were tucking into a breakfast of corn. "Oh, please give me some of your food," he pleaded. "You have so much, and I have nothing."

"I know you," one of the ants cried. "You laughed when I told you to plan ahead. *'Think of the present'* you said. Well, now you can go and find your own food." And the ant turned her back on the grasshopper and cheerfully finished off her breakfast.

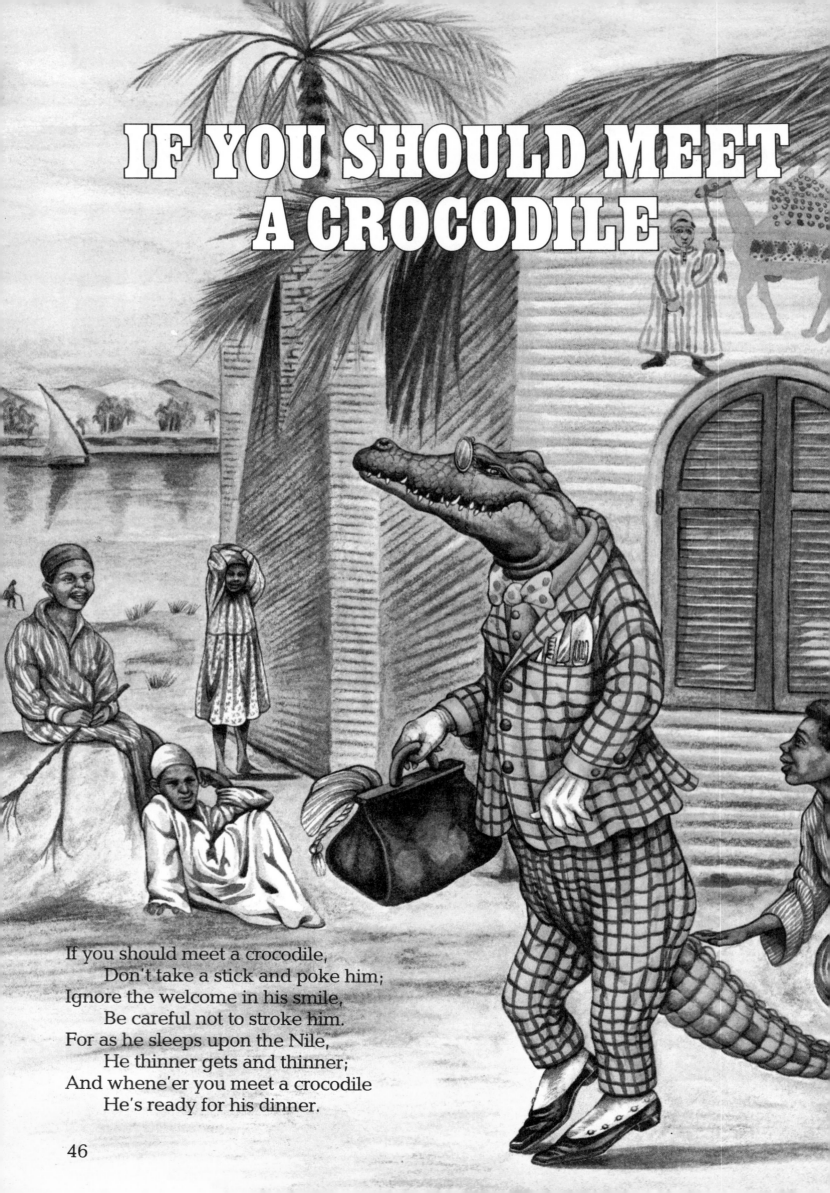

# IF YOU SHOULD MEET A CROCODILE

If you should meet a crocodile,
    Don't take a stick and poke him;
Ignore the welcome in his smile,
    Be careful not to stroke him.
For as he sleeps upon the Nile,
    He thinner gets and thinner;
And whene'er you meet a crocodile
    He's ready for his dinner.

# The Flower Seller

The Flower-seller's fat, and she wears a big shawl!
She sits on the kerb with her basket and all;
The wares that she sells us are not very dear
And are always the loveliest things of the year.
Daffodils in April,
Purple flags in May,
Sweet peas like butterflies
Upon a summer day,
Brown leaves in autumn,
Green leaves in spring,
And berries in the winter
When the carol-singers sing.
The Flower-seller sits with her hands in her lap,
When she's not crying Roses, she's taking a nap;
Her bonnet is queer, and she calls you My dear,
And sells you the loveliest things of the year.

47

# At the Forge

**D**ick and Mary lived on a farm with their parents and their grandpa, and near the farm was the blacksmith's forge. Charles the blacksmith was a great friend of the family.

"Come on, Dick," Mary often said when they had nothing special to do, "let's go and see Charles."

They loved all the sounds of the smithy — the puffing bellows, the clang-clang of the hammer on the anvil, as Charles held the red-hot iron with the long pincers, and hammered it into a horse-shoe. And then the sizzling, as he cooled the hot metal in water.

Dick decided he wanted to become a blacksmith. It seemed so clever to be able to make horse-shoes. Then, one day, Charles let him try to swing the hammer himself. But it was much too heavy — he could hardly lift it. "Cor! how strong a blacksmith has to be!" he thought.

Charles smiled. "Oh, you'll have to grow up a bit, son," he said, as he took back the hammer and swung it easily over his head.

One day old Victor the shire horse lost a shoe. Everyone on the farm was very busy that morning, so Grandpa asked Mary and Dick to take Victor over to the forge to get a new shoe. Mary and Dick were thrilled to be allowed to walk Victor all by themselves.

Charles was busy shoeing someone else's horse when they arrived, so they had to wait. They watched what was going on while Charles pared the horse's hoof and fitted a new shoe.

"Does it hurt, Charles?" asked Dick.

"Oh. No more than it hurts when you cut you nails — if it's done properly, that is."

When he had fitted on the new shoe, he gave the horse a pat. "There you are you patient fellow! You'll be more comfortable now."

Then it was Victor's turn. Victor had been shod so often that Charles had the right size of shoe ready for him. Soon Victor was ready to be taken home.

"Thank you, Charles," said Dick. And just as Grandpa had shown her, Mary took the rein and carefully turned Victor round, walking on the outside of the circle so that his great hoofs did not tread on her.

"Well done, Mary I'll tell your Grandpa he can be really proud of you both."

And Mary and Dick walked Victor slowly back to the farm feeling very pleased with themselves.

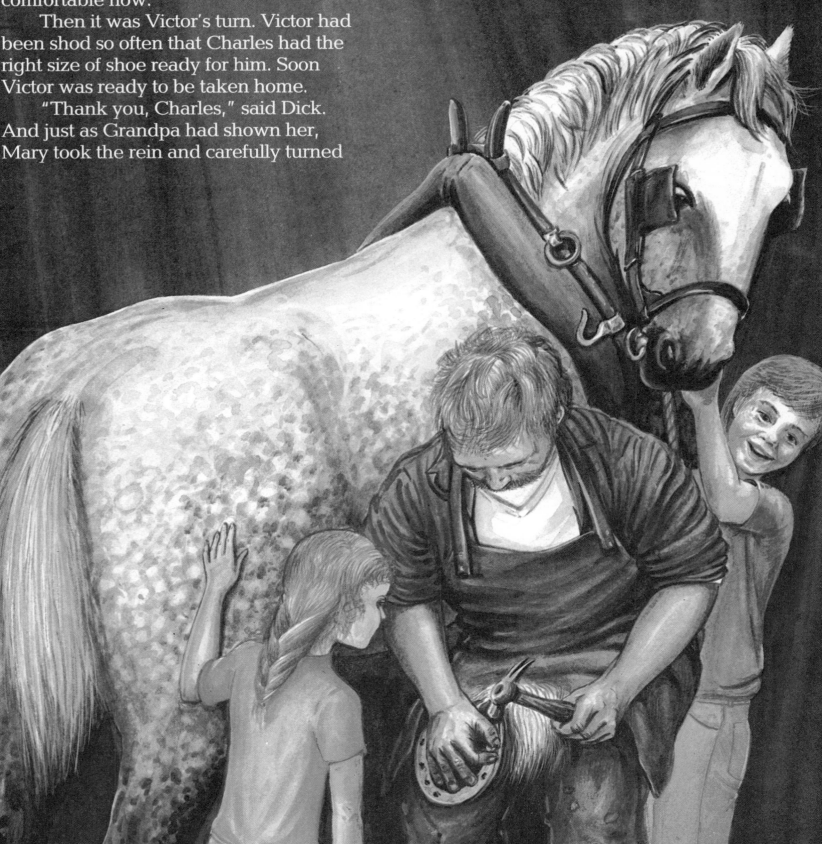

# THE LION AND THE MOUSE

One very hot afternoon, a lion was dozing in a cool, dark cave. He was just about to fall asleep when a mouse scuttled across his nose. With an angry roar, the lion raised his paw and knocked the mouse to the ground. "How dare you wake me up," he snarled. "I'll crush you into the ground."

"O, please, please spare me," squeaked the terrified mouse. "I promise to help you one day if only you'll let me go."

"That's a joke," said the lion. "How could a puny little mouse like you help a big strong lion like me?" And he began to laugh. He laughed so much that he lifted his paw . . . and the mouse escaped.

A few days later the lion was out hunting in the jungle. He was just thinking about his next meal when he tripped over a rope pulled tight across the path. A huge net fell on top of him and, strong as he was, he just could not struggle free. And as he twisted and turned and wriggled and writhed, the net got tighter and tighter.

The lion began to roar so loudly that even the animals outside the jungle could hear him. One of these animals was the little mouse, who was nibbling at a grain of corn. He immediately dropped the corn and ran to the lion. "O mighty lion," he squeaked. "If only you'll keep still I can help you escape."

By now the lion felt so tired that all he could do was lie back and watch as the mouse gnawed through the ropes of the net. He could hardly believe it when some time later he realised he was free.

"You've saved my life, little mouse," he said. "I'll never laugh at the promises made by tiny friends again."

# THE RED NIGHTCAPS

There was once a man who had fifty red nightcaps to sell at a fair. His wife put them in a sack and he set off on his journey.

He travelled along the hot, dusty road until he came to a shady wood. The cool trees looked so inviting that the man threw his sack on the ground and sat down to rest. Then, feeling very sleepy, he took one of the red nightcaps out of the sack, put it on his head, leaned back against a tree and fell fast asleep.

Unknown to the man, a troop of monkeys lived in the wood. After a while a big old monkey crept down a tree and towards the sleeping man.

Very gently he pulled one of the nightcaps out of the sack and popped it on his head. Then he ran back up to the top of the tree and sat there grinning. How monkeys love to copy people! Seeing what the old monkey had done, a young one came swinging down through the trees. He sneaked up to the man, took a nightcap, then ran up to the top of a tree. Then another monkey took a nightcap, then another and another. Soon there were forty-nine monkeys all sitting high in the trees chattering and grinning at each other. And on every head was a new, bright red nightcap! The monkeys made such a noise that the man woke up . . .

and saw the empty sack in front of him. He was in despair.

"Oh, what shall I do?" he cried. "What *shall* I do? What can I say to my wife when I get home without any money — and not even the nightcaps?"

He was so angry with himself for falling asleep that he pulled his red nightcap off and threw it on the ground in a rage.

The forty-nine monkeys sitting high in the trees all saw what the man had done. So, all at once, they pulled off *their* red nightcaps and threw them down on the ground too.

The man just could not believe his good luck. But he was very, very pleased. He picked up the fifty red nightcaps, put them back into his sack, swung it over his shoulder and set off through the woods to sell them at the fair.

# THE FROG, THE CAT AND THE LITTLE RED HEN

At the back of the farmyard, the frog, the cat and the little red hen lived together in a snug wooden house. It was cosy and clean — but no thanks to the frog or the cat! The little red hen did all the work, while *they* lazed in bed. She tidied the house, lit the fire, did the washing and cooked the meals.

"Why don't you get up?" she cried one morning. "The weather's lovely. You could be painting the house or chopping wood or mending the gate." But the frog just turned over and put his head under the covers. And the cat said, "How can I sleep with you squawking?"

Then the little red hen fetched a bag of flour. "Today I'm going to bake a loaf. Who'll light the stove for me?"

"Not me!" yawned the cat, stretching out on the bed.

"Not me!" groaned the frog from under the covers.

So the little red hen fetched wood from the yard and lit the stove, then washed her sooty feathers in the sink.

"Now, who's going to knead the dough for me? It's easy — you just pull it and fold it and press it, like this."

"Not me!"

snapped the cat. "It looks like hard work!"

"Not me!" grumbled the frog. "I didn't see what you did."

So the little red hen kneaded the dough herself and pushed the loaf into the oven. Soon, the glorious smell of baking bread wafted through the house. "Now, who going to fetch the butter?"

"Not me!" sighed the cat.
"I'm still asleep."

leaping out of the bed.

"Oh, please don't trouble yourselves," said the little red hen. Then, tucking the loaf under one wing and the butter under the other, she ran out of the house into the barn.

And she ate the bread all by herself.

"Not me!" moaned the frog. "I'm too tired."

So the little red hen went down to the dairy and asked the cow for her yellow butter. Then she carried it back to the house.

"Now, who will cut the bread for me?" she asked, putting the loaf on the table.

"My paw's sore," wailed the cat.

"I might cut myself," whined the frog.

"But who will help me *eat* the loaf?" asked the little red hen.

"I will!" cried the cat scampering down the ladder.

"So will I! yelled the frog,

# A Child's Thought

At seven, when I go to bed,
I find such pictures in my head:
Castles with dragons prowling round,
Gardens where magic fruits are found;
Fair ladies prisoned in a tower,
Or lost in an enchanted bower;
While gallant horsemen ride by streams
That border all this land of dreams
I find, so clearly in my head
At seven, when I go to bed.

At seven, when I wake again,
The magic land I seek in vain;
A chair stands where the castle frowned,
The carpet hides the garden ground,
No fairies trip across the floor,
Boots, and not horsemen, flank the door,
And where the blue streams rippling ran
Is now a bath and water-can;
I seek the magic land in vain
At seven, when I wake again.

HANNIBAL

Hannibal crossed the Alps,
Hannibal crossed the Alps;
  With his black men, His brown men,
  His countrymen, His townmen,
With his Gauls and his Spaniards,
his horses and elephants,
Hannibal crossed the Alps.

Hannibal crossed the Alps,
Hannibal crossed the Alps;
  For his bow-men, His spear-men
  His front-men, His rear-men,
His Gauls and his Spaniards,
his horses and elephants,
Wanted the Romans scalps!

And that's why
Hannibal, Hannibal, Hannibal,
Hannibal crossed the Alps.

# THE GOOSE THAT LAID THE GOLDEN EGG

A very poor farmer called Edward used to dream all day long about becoming very rich. One morning he was in the milking shed — and dreaming about owning a large herd of cows — when his wife called to him: "Edward, just look what I've found! Oh, this must be the most wonderful day of our lives!"

As he turned to face his wife, Edward rubbed his eyes in disbelief. For there stood his wife, with a goose tucked under her right arm — and a perfect golden egg in her left hand. She laughed happily as she said, "No, no you're not dreaming now. We really *do* have a goose that lays golden eggs. Ooh, just think how rich we'll be if she lays an egg like this every day. We must give her the best treatment possible."

During the weeks that followed that is exactly what they did. Each day they led her to the lush green grass by the village pond, and each night they settled her down on a bed of straw in a warm corner of the kitchen. And not a morning passed

without the appearance of a golden egg.

Edward bought more land and more cows. But he knew he would have to wait a long time before he became *very* rich.

"It's too long," he finally announced one morning. "I'm tired of all this waiting. Our goose obviously has a huge collection of eggs inside her. I think we should take them all out *"now!"*

His wife agreed. She no longer remembered how happy she had been the day she discovered the first golden egg. She handed over a knife and within a few seconds Edward had killed the goose — and cut it open.

Once again he rubbed his eyes in disbelief. But his time his wife didn't laugh, because the dead goose did not contain a single egg. "Oh Edward!" she wailed. "Why were we so greedy? No matter how long we wait, we'll never become rich now."

And from that day on Edward never dreamed about becoming rich again.

# GROWLING AT TIGERS

Once upon a time there was a little Indian boy whose name was Sudi, who loved growling at tigers.

"You be careful," his mother told him. "Tigers don't like being growled at."

But Sudi did not care, and one day, when his mother was out, he went for a walk to find a tiger to growl at.

As soon as Sudi came up the tiger sprang out and growled, "Grrrrr-Grrrrrr-Grrrr-Grrrrrrrrr!" And Sudi growled right back, "Grrrr-Grrrrrr-Grrrrr-Grrrrrrrrr!"

The tiger was annoyed!

"What *does* he think I am?" he thought. "A squirrel? A rabbit? A mouse?"

So the next day, when he saw Sudi coming, he sprang out from behind the tree and growled louder than ever, '*Grrrrrr-Grrrrr-Grrrrr-Grrrrr-Grrrrrr!*"

"Nice tiger! Good boy!" said Sudi, as he stroked him.

The tiger could not bear it and went away and sharped his claws and lashed his tail and practised growling.

"I am a tiger!" he said "T-I-G-E-R: TIGER. GRRRRRRR!" And then he went and had a drink at the pond. When he had finished drinking he looked at his reflection in the water. There he was, a lovely yellow tiger with black stripes and a long tail. He growled again, so loudly that he frightened even himself, and ran away. At last he stopped.

"What am I running away for?"

he thought. "It's only me. Oh dear, that boy has upset me! I wonder why he growls at tigers?"

The next day, when Sudi passed, he stopped him.

"Why do you growl at tigers?" he asked.

"Well," said Sudi, "it's because I'm shy, really. And if I growl at tigers it sort of makes up for it, if you see what I mean."

"Oh, I see!" said the tiger.

"After all, tigers are the fiercest animals in the world and it is very brave to growl at them."

The tiger was pleased.

"Fiercer than lions?"

"Oh yes!" said Sudi.

"And bears?"

"Much fiercer."

The tiger purred and felt friendly.

"You *are* a nice boy!" he said, and gave him a lick.

After that they often went for walks together — and every now and then they growled at each other.

61

# THE LION AND THE PEACOCK

There was once a lion and a peacock who were very great friends. They like nothing better than meeting in a forest clearing on warm, sunny afternoons and eating their food together.

One afternoon, the lion was tearing into huge chunks of meat when he noticed that the peacock was scratching the earth and burying plum stones.

"Surely you can find a better way of spending your time," he said lazily.

Now the peacock was a proud bird who thought he knew everything. "How can you be so stupid?" he asked in amazement. "You must be the only animal in the forest who doesn't know why it's important to plant plum stones. Trees grow from the stones and provide lots of nice, juicy plums."

The lion felt very hurt at being called stupid. "I'll show my friend that I'm as clever as he is." So he carefully buried the bones left over from his meal.

Some weeks later the two friends met again in the same clearing. The peacock was feeling particularly pleased with

himself because the plum stones had begun to sprout. And he laughed when he saw the lion scratching at the ground, anxiously trying to find a bone that had begun to grow.

"You're even more stupid than I thought," he said. "Everyone knows that you can't make bones grow by burying them in the ground."

Time passed and when the two friends met again in the clearing it was full of plum trees laden with fruit. The peacock beamed with pleasure but the lion looked very sad. He had caught nothing to eat that day and would have to go hungry while his friend feasted on rich purple plums.

"It's a pity that you're not as clever as I am," said the peacock proudly. "I'll always have enough to eat while you'll often go hungry."

But the peacock should have known that pride comes before a fall. The lion had had enough of his friend's haughty ways. So, with a quick pounce, he leaped on the peacock and gobbled him up.

# The Moon

The moon has a face like the clock in the hall;
She shines on thieves on the garden wall,
On streets and fields and harbour quays,
And birdies asleep in the forks of the trees.

The squalling cat and the squeaking mouse,
The howling dog by the door of the house,
The bat that lies in the bed at noon,
All love to be out by the light of the moon.

But all of the things that belong to the day
Cuddle to sleep to be out of her way;
And flowers and children close their eyes
Till up in the morning the sun shall arise.